Contents

Facelets Essentials: Guide to JavaServer™ Faces View Definition Framework

by Bruno Aranda and Zubin Wadia

Facelets is a templating language developed from the ground up with JavaServer™ Faces (JSF™) in mind. Because Facelets has come about as a result of many of the concerns with JavaServer™ Pages (JSP™) API when building JSF views, it steps outside of the JSP specification and provides a highly performant, JSF-centric view technology. Its top properties are templating, code reuse, and ease of development.

Focusing on these priorities allows Facelets to help make JSF suitable for large-scale projects. For example, one of the first things a Facelets developer finds is that the technology immediately leads to a reduction in user interface (UI) code. Take our advice: use Facelets in your applications instead of JSP. In this book, we will show you how to maximize your JSF productivity with Facelets by leveraging it the right contexts.

Facelets

When JavaServer Faces (JSF) was devised, the intention was to reuse JSP as the main technology to create pages, as it was already a standard in the web community. The idea was to simplify the adoption of JavaServer Faces by using a familiar tag language that already had a large adoption rate within the Java community.

Unfortunately, JSP and JSF don't naturally complement each other. JSP is used to create static or dynamic web content but not to create component trees. Its elements are processed in a page from top to bottom with the basic objective of creating a response to a request. JSF, however, has a more complex life cycle, and component generation and rendering happen in clearly separated phases. When used together, JSP and JSF both write output to the response, but they do so differently: the JSP container creates output as soon as it finds JSP content, whereas JSF components dictate its own rendering. This difference can cause some problems, as the following code snippet illustrates:

```
<h:outputText value="I am first" />
I am second
```

In this snippet, we mix a JSF tag, the `h:outputText`, with free text (analyzed directly by the JSP container) just after it. As we expect, we get this output in the rendered page:

```
I am first
I am second
```

However, we can encapsulate our previous snippet in a panel (`h:panelGroup`) like so:

```
<h:panelGroup>
      <h:outputText value="I am first"/>
      I am second
</h:panelGroup>
```

If we do, the output is reversed:

```
I am second
I am first
```

We would naturally expect the second snippet to produce output like the first one. However, the JSP container adds the "I am second" text as soon as it encounters it, whereas the h:panelGroup, which is a component that renders its own children, won't produce the "I am first" output until the closing tag is reached.

Problems similar to this can frustrate the developer using JSF for the first time who does not know the implementation details of both JSP and JSF. Facelets fills the gap between JSP and JSF. It is a view technology focused on building component trees and interweaving content with the complex JSF life cycle. Facelets replaces JSP with a very simple API that is a reflection of its simple principles, and it incorporates numerous developer-friendly features, which we describe in the next section.

Why Use Facelets

There are multiple reasons to use Facelets instead of JSP to create JSF pages. First, Facelets does not depend on a web container, so you can use JSF 1.2 without having to use JEE5 or a container that already has JSP 2.1. Facelets can work with any implementation and version of JSF.

Also, as described in the previous section, interweaving JSP and JSF can cause difficulties. In addition, JSTL cannot be used with JSF. Facelets provides a solution for this incompatibility while also providing a compilation process that is much faster than JSP's, because no Java bytecode is actually generated and compiled behind the scenes when you first visit your page.

In addition, Facelets provides templating, so you can reuse your code extensively to simplify the development and maintenance of large-scale applications.

It allows the creation of lightweight components, which are quite trivial to develop compared to the JSF pure components. For example, you don't need to create tags for the UI components.

Then too, Facelets has Unified Expression Language (EL) support, including support for EL functions and compile-time EL validation. The Unified EL takes the features of the JSP EL and adds a few additional capabilities such as deferred expression evaluation, JSTL iteration tags, and method invocation within an expression definition. Facelets also provides precise error reporting, showing detailed information about the line where the exception occurs.

It is possible to use the `jsfc` attribute (which is the equivalent to the `jwcid` concept in Tapestry) to provide integration with existing HTML editors. In the following example, `jsfc` is used to tell the compiler to build a text field component (`h:inputText`) instead of just outputting the `input` tag:

```
<input id="myId" type="text"
jsfc="h:inputText"
value="#{bean.foo}"/>
```

Also, Facelets does not require any special render kits.

Creating an Application with Facelets

In this section, we are going to create a very simple application from scratch that uses Facelets. You will learn how to configure Facelets and get acquainted with some of the basic ideas behind the framework.

Facelets, like JSF, is based on standards and does not depend on any particular operating system or product.

Downloading Facelets

The Facelets project is hosted at Java.net (`http://facelets.dev.java.net/`). There, you can choose the download option that best meets your needs. You can go with the release binary and the sample applications bundled with it, or you can compile from source.

Release Binaries

You can download a release binary from `http://facelets.dev.java.net/servlets/ProjectDocumentList`. Once you've downloaded file, unzip the project into the folder of your choice.

The bundle includes the Facelets JAR at the root level (`jsf-facelets.jar`), and the dependencies can be found in the `lib` folder. Later, we will explain which dependencies Facelets needs.

A few demonstrations are also included; these can be used to start testing the framework. The WAR files for these demonstrations can be found at the root level and their sources in the `demo` folder. Some of the demonstrations follow:

- *starterkit:* A blank Facelets application that can be used when starting an empty project that uses Facelets

- *numberguess:* The traditional demonstration of JSF, where the user needs to guess a number, migrated to Facelets

- *hangman:* Demonstration of a migration from Tapestry to JSF and Facelets

- *portlet:* A small Facelets and MyFaces portlet example that supports the edit and help modes

CVS

You can also check out the source code using CVS if you are a member of Java.net. To do this, execute the following commands, replacing USERNAME with your Java.net login name:

```
cvs -d :pserver:USERNAME@cvs.dev.java.net:/cvs login
cvs -d :pserver:USERNAME@cvs.dev.java.net:/cvs \
    checkout facelets
```

You can find more information on how to check out Facelets from CVS at `http://facelets.dev.java.net/servlets/ProjectSource`.

Maven

The Facelets artifact can be found in the Maven Central Repository (`http://www.ibiblio.org/maven2/`) and in the Java.net Maven Repository (`https://maven-repository.dev.java.net/repository/`). You can include the artifact in your project by adding the following dependency to your Project Object Model (POM):

```
<dependency>
    <groupId>com.sun.facelets</groupId>
    <artifactId>jsf-facelets</artifactId>
    <version>1.1.13</version>
</dependency>
```

Version 1.1.13 is the current one at the time of this writing. You should use a newer version if possible.

Adding Dependencies

Facelets can work with any implementation and version of JSF. It also uses the recent EL API, and it can work with any version or implementation of this API as well. Table 1-1 summarizes the dependencies of Facelets.

Table 1-1. Facelets Dependencies

PROJECT	BUILD	INCLUDED	DESCRIPTION
Apache MyFaces	No	No	Implements JSF 1.1 and JSF 1.2.
JavaServer Faces RI	No	No	The reference implementations of JSF 1.1 and JSF 1.2 are available for use with your application.
JavaServer Faces API	Yes	Yes	JSF 1.2 API that works with the new EL specification. (Optionally, MyFaces Core API could be used.)
EL API	Yes	Yes	The stand-alone EL utilized by both JSP and JSF.
EL RI	No	Yes	The reference implementation that is used by Facelets for handling EL.
Servlet API	Yes	Yes	Servlet API
XML SAX	Yes	No	This dependency should not be an issue for most deployments, as it's a standard part of web containers and JREs.

Creating a Project Structure

Ensuring that your web application has the correct list of libraries included can be one of the trickiest parts when starting a project. Missing libraries or incompatibilities between its versions can lead to obscure exceptions and increase developer frustration. Moreover, the diversity of web containers, each of them with its own libraries and particularities, makes this task even more complex.

If we were to set up a project that uses Facelets and MyFaces, a common directory structure would look like this:

```
$PROJECT
+- /WEB-INF
   +- /lib
      +- /commons-beanutils.jar
      +- /commons-collections.jar
      +- /commons-digester.jar
      +- /commons-logging.jar
      +- /el-api
      +- /el-impl
      +- /jsf-facelets.jar
      +- /myfaces-api.jar
      +- /myfaces-impl.jar
   +- /web.xml
   +- /faces-config.xml
+- /[xhtml documents]
```

The EL libraries (`el-api` and `el-impl`) need to be excluded if the container is JSP 2.1 compliant. JSP 2.1 already contains an EL implementation, and you would have a conflict when starting the application.

If you are using the Reference Implementation (RI), replace `myfaces-api.jar` and `myfaces-impl.jar` with `jsf-ri.jar` and `jsf-api.jar`.

Note   If you're using Maven, you do not need to worry about the dependencies, as Maven will get them for you. You need to declare the JSF implementation in your POM file, though.

Configuring the Web Descriptor (web.xml)

To enable Facelets in your application, you need to configure the `web.xml` file—you need to include the context parameter `javax.faces.DEFAULT_SUFFIX`, which defines the suffix of the documents for your views. By convention, the default extension for pages built using Facelets is `*.xhtml`. The modifications for `web.xml` follow:

```
<web-app>
  . . . . . . . . . . . . . .
  <!-- Use Documents Saved as *.xhtml -->
  <context-param>
    <param-name>javax.faces.DEFAULT_SUFFIX</param-name>
    <param-value>.xhtml</param-value>
  </context-param>
</web-app>
```

Optionally, you can specify other parameters in the web descriptor to further configure the behavior of Facelets. Table 1-2 summarizes the available parameters.

Table 1-2. web.xml Initialization Parameters

PARAMETER	DESCRIPTION
facelets.BUFFER_SIZE	Defines the buffer size to set on the response when the `ResponseWriter` is generated. By default, this value equals −1, which means that no buffer size will be assigned to the response. To ensure that a page is rendered when an error is generated, this value could be increased so the rendered output is not sent to the client before the debug response is generated.
facelets.DECORATORS	List of classes, separated by a semicolon (;), which implement `com.sun.facelets.tag.TagDecorator` and have a no-argument constructor. These decorators will be loaded when the first request hits the `FaceletViewHandler` for page compilation.

PARAMETER	DESCRIPTION
`facelets.DEVELOPMENT`	If this attribute is true, the `FaceletViewHandler` to print out debug information when an error occurs during rendering. This default is false.
`facelets.LIBRARIES`	List of paths to the Facelets tag libraries delimited by a semicolon (;). The paths must be relative to your application's root. These libraries will be loaded when the first request hits the `FaceletViewHandler` for page compilation.
`facelets.REFRESH_PERIOD`	This is the period, in seconds, in which the compiler is checking for changes after a page is requested. Lower values are useful during development, as you can edit your page in a running application, and the page will be compiled. If you don't want the page to be checked for changes, set this parameter to –1. The default is 2.
`facelets.RESOURCE_RESOLVER`	Used to provide a different `ResourceResolver` so other ways to resolve the resources can be implemented. The default is `com.sun.facelets.impl.DefaultResourceResolver`.

Table 1-2. (continued)

PARAMETER	DESCRIPTION
`facelets.SKIP_COMMENTS`	When true, the compiler skips the comments in the page, and nothing within the comments is rendered in the view. When false, although the tags won't be compiled, the EL expressions will be parsed as if they were inline. The default is true.

Configuring the Faces Descriptor (faces-config.xml)

Facelets replaces the default JavaServer Faces `ViewHandler` with its own implementation represented by the class `com.sun.facelets.FaceletViewHandler`. To do this, it takes advantage of JSF's composite nature. To configure our web application to use the Facelets handler instead of the default JSF `ViewHandler`, we need to specify the `<view-handler>` element in the `faces-config.xml` file:

```
<faces-config>
  <application>
    <view-handler>
      com.sun.facelets.FaceletViewHandler
    </view-handler>
  </application>
</faces-config>
```

Creating JSF Views

Now that we have configured the web application, let's create some JSF view documents using Facelets, as a simple example of what Facelets is capable of doing. For more detailed information and the Facelets tag reference, refer to the "Facelets Tag Reference" section.

The Happy Birds Directory

Let's imagine we need to create a simple directory of birds—the Happy Birds Directory—that consists of pages containing information for different birds, with navigation provided by a table of contents. To do this, we decide to create one page per bird, and as a prototype, we'll create the pages for the parrot and the eagle.

As all pages have a similar layout (content and navigation box), we can create a template and define the different areas. Implementing a page for a bird will be a matter of implementing the specific content for that bird.

So, we can create a project structure like the following:

```
$PROJECT
+- /WEB-INF
    +- /lib [with dependencies]
    +- /web.xml
    +- /faces-config.xml
+- template.xhtml
+- index.xhtml
+- parrot.xhtml
+- eagle.xhtml
+- menu.xhtml
```

In WEB-INF, we have the lib folder with dependencies, the web.xml file configured as explained in the previous section, and the faces-config.xml file.

We create five documents (with the extension *.xhtml). One of them is the template (template.xhtml) used by three of the other pages (index.xhtml, parrot.xhtml, and eagle.xhtml). The last page is the menu (menu.xhtml), which we are going to use to navigate through the application.

The Template

In the template, we define the basic layout of the page with the Facelets UI tag `ui:insert`, which we can use to define areas in the page that can be overwritten.

To use the Facelets tags, we need to use the `http://java.sun.com/jsf/facelets` namespace. By convention, we define `ui` as the prefix for the UI Facelets library tags. We need to declare the namespaces for all the tags we are using in a document. If an invalid namespace is provided, Facelets will report an error during compilation.

The code for the template is shown in Listing 1-1.

Listing 1-1. template.xhtml

```
<!DOCTYPE html PUBLIC "-//W3C//DTD
XHTML 1.0 Transitional//EN"
"http://www.w3.org/TR/xhtml1/DTD/ ↪
xhtml1-transitional.dtd">
<html xmlns="http://www.w3.org/1999/xhtml"
      xmlns:ui="http://java.sun.com/jsf/facelets"
      xmlns:f="http://java.sun.com/jsf/core"
      xmlns:h="http://java.sun.com/jsf/html">
<head>
    <title>The Happy Birds Directory</title>

    <style type="text/css">
        <!--
        .box {
            float: right;
            width: 50%;
            border: black dotted 1px;
            padding: 5px
        }
        -->
    </style>
</head>
```

```
<body>
    <h:form>

        <h1>The Happy Birds Directory</h1>

        <div class="box">
            <ui:insert name="navigation"/>
        </div>

        <ui:insert name="main">
            Welcome to the nest!
        </ui:insert>

    </h:form>

</body>
</html>
```

This simple template contains a floating `div` element that we use to render the content table, followed by a main section that describes our birds. The most important elements on this page are the two `ui:insert` tags, named `navigation` and `main`. So, in the template, we declare the `navigation` area inside the `div` element and an open `main` section. In the construction of the other three pages, we will see how we can override these two areas.

We can define default content for the areas just by nesting this content in the `ui:insert` tag. For example, if we don't override the main area, the phrase "Welcome to the nest!" will be shown.

The Home Page

The home page, which is the page that greets the user, is `index.xhtml`. The code for the home page is shown in Listing 1-2.

Listing 1-2. index.xhtml

```
<!DOCTYPE html
        PUBLIC "-//W3C//DTD XHTML ↪
1.0 Transitional//EN"
        "http://www.w3.org/TR/xhtml1/DTD/ ↪
xhtml1-transitional.dtd">
<html xmlns="http://www.w3.org/1999/xhtml"
      xmlns:ui="http://java.sun.com/jsf/facelets"
      xmlns:h="http://java.sun.com/jsf/html">
<body>

This and everything before will be ignored

    <ui:composition template="template.xhtml">

        <ui:define name="navigation">
            <ui:include src="menu.xhtml"/>
        </ui:define>

    </ui:composition>

    This and everything after will be ignored

</body>
</html>
```

Here, we are using three new Facelets tags: `ui:composition`, `ui:define`, and `ui:include`.

We use the `ui:composition` tag's `template` attribute to reference the template we want to use for the page (in our case, the `template.xhtml` document). Everything inside the `ui:composition` tag will be evaluated by Facelets when compiling the document. All elements outside the `ui:composition` tag will be ignored.

We use the `ui:define` tag to define the content that will go in the areas declared in the template. The name attribute of the `ui:define` tag must match the one of the `ui:insert` tag in the template. For the `index.xhtml` view, we only defined the `navigation` area and will use the default `main` area.

In the navigation area, the `ui:include` tag allows us to include the content from another document, in our case, `menu.xhtml`.

The Navigation Menu

As in the home page, we include a menu in the page. The menu is defined in Listing 1-3.

Listing 1-3. menu.xhtml

```
<!DOCTYPE html
        PUBLIC "-//W3C//DTD XHTML 1.0 Transitional//EN"
        "http://www.w3.org/TR/xhtml1/DTD/ ➥
xhtml1-transitional.dtd">
<html xmlns="http://www.w3.org/1999/xhtml"
      xmlns:ui="http://java.sun.com/jsf/facelets"
      xmlns:h="http://java.sun.com/jsf/html">
<body>
This and everything before will be ignored
    <ui:composition>

        <h3>Contents table</h3>
        <hr/>
```

```
<h:panelGrid columns="1">

    <h:commandLink value="Home" action="home" />
    <h:commandLink value="Parrot"
                   action="parrot" />
    <h:commandLink value="Eagle"
                   action="eagle" />

</h:panelGrid>

</ui:composition>
This and everything after will be ignored
</body>
</html>
```

Again, we use the `ui:composition` tags, and everything outside the tags will be removed when the menu is included in a page. This page uses just a few link elements (`h:commandLink`) with `action` attributes defined to trigger the navigation in our application.

We have defined these rules in the `faces-contig.xml` file shown in Listing 1-4.

Listing 1-4. faces-config.xml

```
<!DOCTYPE faces-config PUBLIC
  "-//Sun Microsystems, Inc.//DTD ➥
JavaServer Faces Config 1.0//EN"
  "http://java.sun.com/dtd/web-facesconfig_1_1.dtd" >

<faces-config>

    <application>       <view-handler>
        com.sun.facelets.FaceletViewHandler ➥
        </view-handler>
    </application>

    <navigation-rule>
```

```
        <navigation-case>
            <from-outcome>home</from-outcome>
            <to-view-id>/index.xhtml</to-view-id>
        </navigation-case>
    </navigation-rule>
    <navigation-rule>
        <navigation-case>
            <from-outcome>parrot</from-outcome>
            <to-view-id>/parrot.xhtml</to-view-id>
        </navigation-case>
    </navigation-rule>
    <navigation-rule>
        <navigation-case>
            <from-outcome>eagle</from-outcome>
            <to-view-id>/eagle.xhtml</to-view-id>
        </navigation-case>
    </navigation-rule>
</faces-config>
```

As you can see from the navigation declaration, each link will take the user to one of the pages.

The Bird Pages

The other two pages (parrot.xhtml and eagle.xhtml) are just sample pages showing information for a couple of birds. They are almost identical to the index page, in the sense that they use the template and specify which content to show in the main and navigation parts. The parrot's page is in Listing 1-5.

Listing 1-5. parrot.xhtml

```
<!DOCTYPE html
        PUBLIC "-//W3C//DTD XHTML 1.0 ➥
Transitional//EN"
        "http://www.w3.org/TR/xhtml1/DTD/ ➥
xhtml1-transitional.dtd">
<html xmlns="http://www.w3.org/1999/xhtml"
      xmlns:ui="http://java.sun.com/jsf/facelets"
      xmlns:h="http://java.sun.com/jsf/html">
<body>
This and everything before will be ignored
    <ui:composition template="template.xhtml">

        <ui:define name="navigation">
            <ui:include src="menu.xhtml"/>
        </ui:define>

        <ui:define name="main">

            <h1>Parrot</h1>

            <p>
                Parrots are interesting birds...
            </p>

        </ui:define>
    </ui:composition>

 This and everything after will be ignored

</body>
</html>
```

This time, we put a description of the parrot in the main area by using the ui:define tag and matching its name with the one in the ui:insert tag of the template. The navigation area just includes the menu, as on the index page.

And, we have a similar page for the eagle in Listing 1-6.

Listing 1-6. eagle.xhtml

```
<!DOCTYPE html
        PUBLIC "-//W3C//DTD XHTML 1.0 Transitional//EN"
        "http://www.w3.org/TR/xhtml1/DTD/ ↪
xhtml1-transitional.dtd">
<html xmlns="http://www.w3.org/1999/xhtml"
      xmlns:ui="http://java.sun.com/jsf/facelets"
      xmlns:h="http://java.sun.com/jsf/html">
<body>
This and everything before will be ignored
    <ui:composition template="template.xhtml">

        <ui:define name="navigation">
            <ui:include src="menu.xhtml"/>

        <p>An eagle flying high...</p>
        </ui:define>

        <ui:define name="main">

            <h1>Eagle</h1>

            <p>
                Eagles are bigger than parrots.
            </p>

        </ui:define>
    </ui:composition>

This and everything after will be ignored

</body>
</html>
```

This page is almost identical to the parrot one, except for implementing the eagle-specific content. We could add more and more pages to describe different birds and just implement different information for each bird without having to alter the layout.

Of course, this simple version of the Happy Birds Directory could also be implemented using a database and some managed beans, but we wanted to illustrate the most important capabilities of the templating in Facelets.

Migrating an Existing Application from JSP to Facelets

Migrating an existing application that uses JSP for its views to Facelets is pretty straightforward. To summarize, the needed steps are:

1. Include the Facelets JAR and its dependencies.

2. Change the page declaration of your pages from

   ```
   <%@ taglib uri=http://java.sun.com/jsf/html
           prefix="h"%>
   <%@ taglib uri=http://java.sun.com/jsf/core
           prefix="f"%>
   ```

   to

   ```
   <html xmlns="http://www.w3.org/1999/xhtml"
           xmlns:h="http://java.sun.com/jsf/html"
           xmlns:f="http://java.sun.com/jsf/core">
   ```

3. Verify and validate your documents, so they are XHTML compliant (e.g., all the tags are properly closed).

And now you can forget about some of the headaches you had when using JSP with JSF!

Unified Expression Language

The Unified Expression Language was successfully created in an attempt to align the Expression Languages (ELs) used in JSP 2.0 and JSF 1.1. The Unified EL allowed expressions to be evaluated in a deferred manner, versus immediately in the original EL. In JSF, immediate evaluation would be OK the first time a page is rendered, but on postback, that page must be evaluated in the different phases of the cycle (not only in the rendering). JSF needs to convert the values resulting from the expressions, validate them, bind them to server-side components, use them to process events, and so on.

There are other differences between the two ELs. The classic JSP EL can use functions, which are calls to static methods that can be defined in the top-level domain (TLD). However, support for functions didn't go into the JSF EL, because functions cannot be used to dynamically invoke methods on objects.

Also, each of the EL versions uses different syntax for its expressions. JSP EL uses `${. . .}`, and JSF EL uses `#{. . .}`.

Because of these differences, the JSF and JSP versions of the EL are not compatible and cannot be mixed in a page. The following piece of code would render an unexpected response when using JSF 1.1 and JSP 2.0:

```
<c:forEach var="bird" items="${directoryBean.birds}">
<h:inputText id="empName" value="#{bird.name}" />
 </c:forEach>
```

In this example, as `c:forEach` is only evaluated during rendering of the page, the employee variable is not available during the other phases of the JSF life cycle. Therefore, the value of the `h:inputText` component will never be updated in the model. Moreover, the previous example would throw an exception when duplicate IDs are found, as JSF would try to create a new h:inputText component, with the same ID, for each iteration.

The ELs defined by JSF 1.1 and JSP 2.0 have been integrated into the new Unified Expression Language. Thanks to the Unified EL, JSTL tags, such as the iteration tags, can now be used intuitively with JSF components.

Facelets uses the new Unified EL. It supports the use of ${. . .} and #{. . .} syntax and makes no distinction between the two. Therefore, you can use either one, depending on the developer's particular taste.

Inline Text

With Facelets, you can insert an EL expression anywhere in the page, so the expression can appear in line with text without using a component to output the value referenced by the expression. For instance, the following code will be correctly evaluated when rendering the document:

```
<p>The Happy Birds Directory
    contains #{directoryBean.totalCount} birds.
</p>
```

Tag Libraries

As illustrated in our sample application, Facelets needs valid XML with namespace support for compilation. To use a tag library in our page, we must declare it by using its namespace. We can do that by mapping the library's URI (or URL) to a prefix.

For example, take a look at this document:

```
<!DOCTYPE html PUBLIC "-//W3C//DTD ↪
XHTML 1.0 Transitional//EN"
        "http://www.w3.org/TR/xhtml1/DTD/ ↪
xhtml1-transitional.dtd">
<html xmlns="http://www.w3.org/1999/xhtml"
        xmlns:ui="http://java.sun.com/jsf/facelets"
        xmlns:h="http://java.sun.com/jsf/html">
```

```
<body>
    <ui:composition>
            <h:outputText value="#{bird.name}" />
    </ui:composition>
</body>
</html>
```

In this example, we are using three libraries: one for XHTML without a prefix; one for the Facelets tags with the `ui` prefix; and another one for the JSF basic HTML tags, with the `h` prefix.

In the Table 1-3 we summarize the namespaces for some of the most common libraries:

Table 1-3. Library Namespaces

NAMESPACE	PREFIX	LIBRARY
`http://www.w3.org/1999/xhtml`	`--`	XHTML
`http://java.sun.com/jsf/facelets`	`ui`	Facelets Templating
`http://java.sun.com/jsf/core`	`f`	JSF Core
`http://java.sun.com/jsf/html`	`h`	JSF HTML
`http://myfaces.apache.org/tomahawk`	`t`	MyFaces Tomahawk
`http://myfaces.apache.org/sandbox`	`s`	MyFaces Tomahawk Sandbox
`http://myfaces.apache.org/trinidad`	`tr`	MyFaces Trinidad
`http://java.sun.com/jstl/core`	`c`	JSTL Core
`http://java.sun.com/jsp/jstl/fmt`	`fn`	JSTL Functions

If you put a tag in your page that contains the prefix to a namespace that is not specified in any tag library, the tag will be ignored and treated as text by the compiler. If this happens, you won't see any output in the rendered page unless you verify the rendered source code. In most cases, a lack of rendered output means that the namespace has been incorrectly typed in the page or the tag library has not been found.

Also, you could be using a tag with a known namespace, but the tag is missing from the library. In this case, the compiler will throw an exception.

Loading the Tag Libraries

Facelets uses a couple of strategies to load tag libraries. First, it searches the classpath trying to find libraries in the `/META-INF` folder of the JAR files. It will try to load any file that has the extension `*.taglib.xml`. For instance, this is how the templating library is loaded from the Facelets binaries.

After the `/META-INF` folder, Facelets will check the libraries defined in the `web.xml` file with the initialization parameter `facelets.LIBRARIES`. This strategy is useful when creating tag libraries that are specific to your web application.

Available Libraries

Several tag libraries are already included in the Facelets binaries:

Templating library: This contains the tags using for templating, which was shown in the previous example and will be explained in more detail in the "Facelets Tag Reference" section.

JSF libraries: The two tag libraries for the JavaServer Faces specification are supported by default by Facelets. They contain all the necessary information to allow you to use JSF tags in your documents the same way you would do in JSP.

JSTL: Facelets provides partial support for JavaServer Pages Standard Tag Library (JSTL) tags. While the Function library is fully supported, the Core tags are only partially so. The Core tags supported by Facelets are: `c:if`, `c:forEach`, `c:catch`, and `c:set`.

Note   In this JSTL implementation, all EL variables used in the implemented JSTL tags are backed by the new EL API. Their scope is limited to the current `FaceletContext` and no others. Hence, those variables exist only for the purpose of creating the component tree and do not work to assign variables in other scopes. The reason behind this is that the EL expressions are actually bound to the `FaceletContext` and not the evaluated `Object`.

Other Tag Libraries

Other component libraries, such as MyFaces Trinidad, already support Facelets out of the box, as they include the Facelets tag library file in the `/META-INF` folder of the JAR.

However, at the time of this writing, the MyFaces Tomahawk library and its sandbox are not included in that library. When we want to use Tomahawk, we will need to specifically import the `taglib` file into our application. The MyFaces wiki pages contain the most up-to-date information on how to use Tomahawk with Facelets; see `http://wiki.apache.org/myfaces/Use_Facelets_with_Tomahawk`.

Creating a Tag Library

If you want to use other libraries that do not have a Facelets tag library, you will need to create the tag library file yourself and register it in your `web.xml` file. In this XML document, you need to specify the namespace for the tags and define every tag.

For example, to illustrate how to register the tags, we can use the limited tag library implementation for Tomahawk shown in Listing 1-7.

Listing 1-7. tomawawk-partial.taglib.xml

```xml
<!DOCTYPE facelet-taglib PUBLIC
   "-//Sun Microsystems, Inc.//DTD Facelet ↪
Taglib 1.0//EN"
   "http://java.sun.com/dtd/facelet-taglib_1_0.dtd">

<facelet-taglib>
 <namespace>http://myfaces.apache.org/tomahawk
</namespace>

<tag>
        <tag-name>inputCalendar</tag-name>
        <component>
            <component-type>
                org.apache.myfaces.HtmlInputCalendar
            </component-type>
            <renderer-type>org.apache.myfaces.Calendar
            </renderer-type>
        </component>
   </tag>
 <tag>
        <tag-name>saveState</tag-name>
        <component>
            <component-type>
                org.apache.myfaces.SaveState
            </component-type>
        </component>
   </tag>
 <facelet-taglib>
```

This library only would only be supporting the `t:inputCalendar` and `t:saveState` components. Of course, this implementation of the Tomahawk library would be a very limited, but you can see the MyFaces wiki pages for a more comprehensive implementation. Every Facelets `taglib` must contain the namespace for the tags followed by the listing of tags (and functions, as you will see later).

Facelets uses a simple document type definition (DTD) to describe the library files:

```
<!ELEMENT facelet-taglib (libraryclass| ↪
(namespace,(tag|function)+))>
<!ATTLIST facelet-taglib xmlns
CDATA #FIXED
"http://java.sun.com/JSF/Facelet">
<!ELEMENT namespace (#PCDATA)>
<!ELEMENT library-class (#PCDATA)>
<!ELEMENT tag (tag-name,(handler- ↪
class|component|converter ↪
|validator|source))>
<!ELEMENT tag-name (#PCDATA)>
<!ELEMENT handler-class (#PCDATA)>
<!ELEMENT component (component-type, ↪
renderer-type?,handler-class?)>
<!ELEMENT component-type (#PCDATA)>
<!ELEMENT renderer-type (#PCDATA)>
<!ELEMENT converter (converter-id, handler-class?)>
<!ELEMENT converter-id (#PCDATA)>
<!ELEMENT validator (validator-id, handler-class?)>
<!ELEMENT validator-id (#PCDATA)>
<!ELEMENT source (#PCDATA)>
<!ELEMENT function (function-name, ↪
function-class,function-signature)>
<!ELEMENT function-name (#PCDATA)>
<!ELEMENT function-class (#PCDATA)>
<!ELEMENT function-signature (#PCDATA)>
```

Here, we can use the `library-class` element to delegate the definition of the library. This class must implement `com.sun.facelets.tag.TagLibrary`, which is useful when you want to maintain your library from Java.

If you are not using the library-class element, you must specify a namespace. You will use this namespace in your documents as explained in the beginning of this section. In the rest of the document, you will find the tags and functions.

Remember to register the tag library in the web descriptor file (web.xml), if the tag library was not already included in a JAR. Add the library under the parameter facelets.LIBRARIES, and separate multiple libraries with semicolons.

Functions

In the tag libraries, you can declare functions, which are invocations of Java static methods. For example, you could have Listing 1-8 in the taglib file:

Listing 1-8. bird-functions.taglib.xml

```
<!DOCTYPE facelet-taglib PUBLIC
  "-//Sun Microsystems, Inc.//DTD
Facelet Taglib 1.0//EN"
  "http://java.sun.com/dtd/facelet-taglib_1_0.dtd">

<facelet-taglib>
 <namespace>http://myfaces.apress.com/birds</namespace>

<function>
        <function-name>isBirdAbleToSpeak</function-name>
        <function-class>
           com.apress.myfaces.BirdFunctions
```

```
        </function-class>
        <function-signature>java.lang.String
canSpeak(java.lang.String
canSpeak(java.lang.String))
</function-signature>
 </function>
</facelet-taglib>
```

In this library, we have defined only one function (though we can define as many as we want) that calls the method with the signature `String canSpeak(String)` from the `BirdFunctions` class. The `BirdFunctions` class is shown in Listing 1-9.

Listing 1-9. BirdFunctions.java

```java
package com.apress.myfaces;

public class BirdFunctions {

    public static String canSpeak(String birdName) {
        if (birdName.equals("parrot")) {
            return "YES";
        }
        return "If you try hard enough, who knows!";
    }
}
```

Functions are part of the EL specification, so we could use the previous function in our JSF views, like in the following snippet:

```html
<!DOCTYPE html PUBLIC "-//W3C//DTD
        XHTML 1.0 Transitional//EN"
        "http://www.w3.org/TR/xhtml1/DTD/ ➥
        xhtml1-transitional.dtd">
<html xmlns="http://www.w3.org/1999/xhtml"
      xmlns:b="http://myfaces.apress.com/birds">
<body>
    Parrots can speak:
#{b:isBirdAbleToSpeak('parrot')} <br/>
```

```
    Eagles can speak: #{b:isBirdAbleToSpeak('eagle')}
</body></html>
```

And this simple page, which includes two uses of our function, would render the following:

```
Parrots can speak: YES
Eagles can speak: If you try hard enough, who knows!
```

The jsfc Attribute

Like the Apache Tapestry framework, Facelets provides a way to convert an XML tag into another at compile time via the `jsfc` attribute. This attribute can be used to create tags for rendering by visual tools and convert them to another tag. A typical `jsfc` example follows:

```
<!DOCTYPE html PUBLIC "-//W3C//DTD ↪
XHTML 1.0 Transitional//EN"
"http://www.w3.org/TR/xhtml1/DTD/ ↪
xhtml1-transitional.dtd">
<html xmlns="http://www.w3.org/1999/xhtml"
      xmlns:h="http://java.sun.com/jsf/html">

<body>
  <input type="text" jsfc="h:inputText"
                    value="#{bird.name}" />
</body>
</html>
```

Compiling this code will convert the input tag into an `h:inputText` component so we can use its JSF features.

Although using `jsfc` is more limiting than using the JSF components, it can help to accommodate page authoring needs. Many designers are used to authoring pages using visual tools that generate HTML code; with the `jsfc` attribute, they can continue using these tools. By simply decorating the HTML with the `jsfc` attribute, they can take advantage of JSF as well.

When using `jsfc`, the same rules for namespaces and naming apply to the `jsfc` attribute value.

Facelets Templating and Template Clients

Using templates helps you to meet some of the major goals of developing web applications. Templates allow you to reuse more code, thus reducing the development and maintenance costs of an application. Moreover, templates help to achieve a common look and feel, as all pages using a specific template will look similar.

Facelets templates can be created from both JSF components and HTML tags. Templates can be interwoven thanks to the fact that they are compiled during the render phase.

We distinguish in Facelets between templates and template clients. The latter use the templates to create variations of the same pattern.

A template defines spots where the content can be replaced. Which content is used in those spots is defined by the clients. The template defines the different areas using the `ui:insert` tag, and the clients use the templates with `ui:component`, `ui:composition`, `ui:fragment`, or `ui:decorate` tags.

Templating in Facelets is not just limited to one level. It is possible to have multilevel templating, as a client for one template can be a template for other client templates. Hence, Facelets powerful templating support allows you to create complex composite applications.

In the next section, we go over all the UI tags in Facelets, alphabetically.

Facelets Tag Reference

We'll now describe all of the tags available in the Facelets library and explain each one's attributes. Some of the tags for templating have been introduced in previous examples, but we'll include them here too, so you have a complete reference.

<ui:component/>

The `ui:component` tag inserts a new `UIComponent` instance into the JavaServer Faces tree as the root of all the components or content fragments it contains. Table 1-4 shows its attributes.

Table 1-4. UI Component Attributes

ATTRIBUTE NAME	REQUIRED	DESCRIPTION
id	No	As with any component, an `id` can be provided. If none is present, Facelets will create an `id` following the JavaServer specification rules.
binding	No	Following the JavaServer specification, this attribute can be used to reference a `UIComponent` instance by pointing to a property of managed bean. The instance will be lazily created if the property did not have an instance assigned already.

Everything outside of this component's tags will be ignored by the compiler and won't appear on the rendered view:

```
This and everything before this will be ignored.
<ui:component binding="#{backingBean.myComponent}">
  <div>The directory contains #{totalBirds} birds!</div>
</ui:component>
This and everything after this will be ignored.
```

The preceding code will produce this HTML output:

```
<div>The directory contains 214 birds!</div>
```

<ui:composition/>

The `ui:composition` tag is a templating tag used to encapsulate content that can be included in other Facelets pages. Table 1-5 shows its attribute.

Table 1-5. UI Composition Attribute

ATTRIBUTE NAME	REQUIRED	DESCRIPTION
template	No	The path to the template that will be populated by the content between the start and end of the composition tag.

This tag is a fundamental piece in Facelets and is based in the idea of compositions. The `UIComponent` tree may be formed by compositions described in different pages across the application. Like the `ui:component` tag, everything before and after the composition tag will be removed; the difference between these two tags is that this tag does not create a component in the tree.

```
This and everything before this will be ignored.
<ui:composition>
  <h:outputText value="#{bird.lifeExpectancy}" />
</ui:composition>

This and everything after this will be ignored.
```

We can use the composition tag to populate a template, as shown in the example from the "Creating JSF Views" section. We could use something like this:

```
<ui:composition template="bird-template.xhtml">
    <ui:define name="summary">
        <h:panelGrid columns="2">
            <h:outputText value="Bird Name"/>
            <h:outputText value="#{bird.name}"/>
```

```
            <h:outputText value="Life expectancy"/>
         <h:outputText
            value="#{bird.lifeExpectancy}"/>
         </h:panelGrid>
      </ui:define>
   </ui:composition>
```

The content within the composition tag would be used to populate the
`ui:insert` tag with name `summary` from the `bird-template.xhtml`
template.

The major players where creating composite views with Facelets are the
`ui:composition`, `ui:define`, and `ui:insert` tags. The latter two are
explained later in this section.

<ui:debug/>

The debug tag is a very useful tool when developing an application. When
launched using the combination Ctrl + Shift + <hot key> (D, by default), it
will display a pop-up window that shows the component tree and the
scoped variables. Table 1-6 shows its attributes.

Table 1-6. UI Debug Attributes

ATTRIBUTE NAME	REQUIRED	DESCRIPTION
hotkey	No	Pressing Ctrl + Shift + <hot key> will display the Facelets debug window. This attribute cannot be an EL expression. The default value is d.
rendered	No	Following the JavaServer Faces specification, this attribute must evaluate to a Boolean value. If it is false, the script needed to launch the debug window won't be present in the page.

Conventionally, the debug tag can be found at the end of the pages, but it
can be used anywhere. We can use the debug tag as in this example:

```
<ui:debug hotkey="g"
      rendered="#{initParam['apress.DEBUG_MODE']}"/>
```

In this case, the debug window will be launched when pressing Ctrl + Shift + G and would be rendered if our `init` parameter with name `apress.DEBUG_MODE` is set to true. Usually, we don't want the debug script rendered when in production, so it is convenient to have a single point of configuration (like in the previous example), so we can enable or disable all debug tags.

\<ui:decorate/>

The `ui:decorate` tag is similar to the `ui:composition` tag, the only difference being that the decorate tag does not remove everything outside of it. As its names implies, you can use this tag to add some content around the decorated section by using a template. Table 1-7 shows its attribute.

Table 1-7. UI Decorate Attribute

ATTRIBUTE NAME	REQUIRED	DESCRIPTION
template	Yes	The path to the template that will be populated by the content between the start and end of the composition tag

For instance, we would have a template that wraps the content of the decorate tag in a box creating using `div` elements, like the one in Listing 1-10.

Listing 1-10. box-template.xhtml

```
<!DOCTYPE html PUBLIC "-//W3C//DTD ➥
XHTML 1.0 Transitional//EN"
       "http://www.w3.org/TR/xhtml1/DTD/ ➥
xhtml1-transitional.dtd">
<html xmlns="http://www.w3.org/1999/xhtml"
       xmlns:ui="http://java.sun.com/jsf/facelets">
```

```
<body>

<ui:composition>
    <div style="border: 1px solid black; display:block">
      <ui:insert name="header"/>
    </div>
    <div style="border: 1px solid black; display:block">
        <ui:insert name="content"/>
    </div>
</ui:composition>
</body>
</html>
```

Once we have the template, we could use the decorate tag as shown in Listing 1-11:

Listing 1-11. decorate-example.xhtml

```
<!DOCTYPE html
     PUBLIC "-//W3C//DTD XHTML 1.0 Transitional//EN"
     "http://www.w3.org/TR/xhtml1/DTD/ ➥
xhtml1-transitional.dtd">
<html xmlns="http://www.w3.org/1999/xhtml"
      xmlns:ui="http://java.sun.com/jsf/facelets"
      xmlns:h="http://java.sun.com/jsf/html">
  <head>
       <title>Decorate example</title>
  </head>
  <body>

  <p>These are the birds in today's menu:</p>

  <ui:decorate template="box-template.xhtml">
     <ui:define name="header">
        Happy Parrot
     </ui:define>
     <ui:define name="content">
        How many parrots do you want?
        <h:inputText value="3"/>
```

```
        </ui:define>
    </ui:decorate>
    <br/>
    <ui:decorate template="box-template.xhtml">
        <ui:define name="header">
            Mighty Eagle
        </ui:define>
        <ui:define name="content">
            Eagles are not available now.
        </ui:define>
    </ui:decorate>
    </body>
</html>
```

In the preceding listing, we would create a page and include two boxes with bird information. Everything outside the page will be rendered in the final page, and we would end up with HTML output like the following:

```
<html xmlns="http://www.w3.org/1999/xhtml">
  <head>
        <title>Decorate example</title>
  </head>
  <body>

  <p>These are the birds in today's menu:</p>
    <div style="border: 1px solid black; display:block">

            Happy Parrot
    </div>
    <div style="border: 1px solid black; display:block">
            How many parrots do you want?
      <input id="_id6" name="_id6"
            type="text" value="3" />
    </div>

  <br/>
    <div style="border: 1px solid black; display:block">
            Mighty Eagle
```

```
    </div>

    <div style="border: 1px solid black; display:block">
        Eagles are not available now.
    </div>
```

As you can see in the rendered page, the `div` tags that create the boxes frame the content defined in the decorate tag.

Note too that the template uses `ui:composition` tags to trim everything outside them. Otherwise, when we used this template with a decorate tag, the HTML and body tags would be repeated in the final output.

<ui:define/>

The `ui:define` templating tag can be used to insert named content into a template. It can be used within tags that allow templating, such as the `ui:composition` and `ui:decorate` tags. The names used in the define tag must match the names used in the `ui:insert` tags in the target template. Table 1-8 shows its attribute.

Table 1-8. UI Define Attribute

ATTRIBUTE NAME	REQUIRED	DESCRIPTION
name	Yes	This mandatory attribute specifies the literal name of the definition. It must match with the name of a `ui:insert` tag in the target template.

Let's take a look at the following snippet:

```
<ui:decorate template="box-template.xhtml">
    <ui:define name="header">
        Happy Parrot
    </ui:define>

    this will be removed
```

```
        <ui:define name="content">
             How many parrots do you want?
        </ui:define>
    </ui:decorate>
```

The template used by this snippet contains to insert tags, named `header` and `content`. The code within the define tags will be inserted in those areas, matching by name.

The content outside the define tags will be ignored by the Facelets compiler.

Listing 1-12 illustrates the define tag in action.

Listing 1-12. define-template.xhtml

```
<h:outputText value="Which bird sings like this? "/>
<ui:insert name="song"/>
define-example.xhtml
This will be ignored
<ui:composition template="define-template.xhtml">
        <ui:define name="song">
<h:outputText value="cock-a-doodle-doo"/>
        </ui:define>
</ui:composition>
```

This example will render

```
Which bird sings like this? cock-a-doodle-doo
```

<ui:fragment/>

The `ui:fragment` tag is similar to the `ui:component` tag, but the fragment tag does not trim the content outside itself. Table 1-9 shows its attributes.

Table 1-9. UI Fragment Attributes

Attribute Name	Required	Description
id	No	As with any component, an `id` can be provided. If none is present, Facelets will create an `id` following the JavaServer specification rules.
binding	No	Following the JavaServer specification, this attribute can be used to reference a `UIComponent` instance by pointing to a property of managed bean. The instance will be lazily created if the property did not have an instance assigned already.

The fragment tag inserts a new `UIComponent` instance into the component tree, and any other components or content fragments outside the tag will still be included at compile time. All elements with the fragment tag will be added as children of the component instance.

```
This will be ignored
<ui:fragment>
    <div>
        <h:outputText
            value="I want #{eagle.total} eagles."/>
    </div>
</ui:fragment>
This will be ignored
```

This will create the following output:

```
This will be ignored
    <div>I want 3 eagles.</div>
This will be ignored
```

<ui:include/>

The `ui:include` tag can be used to include another Facelets file into your document. It simply includes whatever source file you specify. You can include any Facelets file that has `ui:component` or `ui:composition` tags (which trim the content outside themselves) or simply a fragment of XHTML or XML. Table 1-10 shows its attribute.

Table 1-10. UI Include Attribute

Attribute Name	Required	Description
src	Yes	This attribute can be a literal value or an EL expression that declares the target Facelets to be included in the document.

The path in the `src` attribute can be absolute or relative. If it is relative, it will be resolved against the original Facelets that was requested.

```
<div>
  <ui:include src="#{backingBean.currentMenu}"/>
</div>
```

In this example, the expression `#{backingBean.currentMenu}` will be resolved to a file path. This can be use to include content dynamically depending on the context.

\<ui:insert/\>

The `ui:insert` tag is used to specify in a template those parts that can be replaced by `ui:define` tags declared in the client template. Table 1-11 shows its attribute.

Table 1-11. UI Insert Attribute

Attribute Name	Required	Description
name	No	This name will be use to match the insert tag with the same name in the client for the template. If no name is specified, the whole client template will be inserted.

The insert tag can contain nested content. If this is the case and no define tag is specified in the client that matches the name of the insert tag, the nested content will be inserted. It can be used to insert default content when the define tag is not specified.

Let's take a look at the example in Listing 1-13.

Listing 1-13. insert-template.xhtml

```
<!DOCTYPE html PUBLIC "-//W3C//DTD ↪
XHTML 1.0 Transitional//EN"
        "http://www.w3.org/TR/xhtml1/DTD/ ↪
xhtml1-transitional.dtd">
<html xmlns="http://www.w3.org/1999/xhtml"
      xmlns:ui="http://java.sun.com/jsf/facelets">
<body>
    <h1>
        <ui:insert name="title">
            No title
        </ui:insert>
    </h1>

    <div>
        <ui:insert name="content">
            No content is defined
        </ui:insert>
    </div>
</body>
</html>
```

We'll need a client for this template; see Listing 1-14.

Listing 1-14. insert-client.xhtml

```
<ui:composition template="insert-template.xhtml">
        <ui:define name="title">
            The Parrot Quest
        </ui:define>
    </ui:composition>
```

In this client Facelets application, we have only defined the `title`, so the `content` will be the default value. Given that, we expect the following output:

```
<h1>
        The Parrot Quest
  </h1>
<div>
          No content is defined
</div>
```

The `name` attribute of the insert tag is optional, and when it is not present, the whole client template will be inserted, and then it is not necessary to use define tags in the client. Let see this with the new example in Listings 1-15 and 1-16.

Listing 1-15 contains the code for a template that contains a `ui:insert` tag without attributes or children:

Listing 1-15. insert-template2.xhtml

```
<!DOCTYPE html PUBLIC "-//W3C//DTD ↪
HTML 1.0 Transitional//EN"
        "http://www.w3.org/TR/xhtml1/DTD/ ↪
xhtml1-transitional.dtd">
<html xmlns="http://www.w3.org/1999/xhtml"
      xmlns:ui="http://java.sun.com/jsf/facelets">
<body>
    <div>
        <h1>One story of Birds</h1>
        <ui:insert/>
    </div>
</body>
</html>
```

In Listing 1-16, we show how to use the previous template to include some content.

Listing 1-16. insert-client2.xhtml

```
<ui:composition template="insert-template2.xhtml">
        One day I decided to start counting
        the number of parrots in the world,
        just to find that...
        <br/>
        <h:inputTextarea value="#{backingBean.story}"/>
  </ui:composition>
```

In this case, the whole content of the composition in `insert-client2.xhtml` will be inserted where the insert tag has been placed in the template. The output will be as follows:

```
<div>
        <h1>One story of Birds</h1>
        One day I decided to start counting
        the number of parrots in the world,
        just to find that...
        <br />
        <textarea name="_id3"></textarea>
</div>
```

<ui:param/>

Until now, we have been seeing how Facelets can pass fragments of code between documents. But we can also pass objects using the `ui:param` tag. This tag is used to pass objects as named variables between Facelets. Table 1-12 shows its attributes.

Table 1-12. UI Param Attributes

ATTRIBUTE NAME	REQUIRED	DESCRIPTION
name	Yes	The name of the variable to pass to the included Facelets
value	Yes	The literal or EL expression value to assign to the named variable

The `name` attribute of the `ui:param` tag must match the name of a `ui:define` tag contained in the template defined in the `ui:composition` or `ui:decorate` tag. Listing 1-17 shows an example.

Listing 1-17. param-details.xhtml

```
<!DOCTYPE html PUBLIC "-//W3C//DTD XHTML 1.0
Transitional//EN"
        "http://www.w3.org/TR/xhtml1/DTD/xhtml1-
transitional.dtd">
<html xmlns="http://www.w3.org/1999/xhtml"
      xmlns:ui="http://java.sun.com/jsf/facelets">
<body>
    <ui:composition>
        <div>
            <h3>#{birdName}</h3>
            Order: #{birdOrder}
            <br/>
            Family: #{birdFamily}
        </div>
    </ui:composition>
</body>
</html>
```

We use the previous Facelets file in the following application in Listing 1-18.

Listing 1-18. param-example.xhtml

```
<!DOCTYPE html PUBLIC "-//W3C//DTD ↪
XHTML 1.0 Transitional//EN"
        "http://www.w3.org/TR/xhtml1/DTD/ ↪
xhtml1-transitional.dtd">
<html xmlns="http://www.w3.org/1999/xhtml"
      xmlns:ui="http://java.sun.com/jsf/facelets">
<body>
    <ui:include src="param-details.xhtml">
        <ui:param name="birdName" value="Parrot"/>
        <ui:param name="birdOrder"
```

```
                    value="Psittaciformes"/>
        <ui:param name="birdFamily"
                    value="Psittacidae"/>
    </ui:include>

    <ui:decorate template="param-details.xhtml">
        <ui:param name="birdName" value="Eagle"/>
        <ui:param name="birdOrder"
                    value="Falconiformes"/>
        <ui:param name="birdFamily"
                    value="Accipitridae"/>
    </ui:decorate>
</body>
</html>
```

In this example, we are using `ui:param` to pass several literals (we could have referred to other objects using EL expressions) to the included document or to a template (in our example, both point to the same Facelets file: `param.details.xhtml`). The resulting relevant output follows:

```
<div>
            <h3>Parrot</h3>
            Order: Psittaciformes
            <br />
            Family: Psittacidae
</div>
<div>
            <h3>Eagle</h3>
            Order: Falconiformes
            <br />
            Family: Accipitridae
</div>
```

<ui:remove/>

The `ui:remove` tag is used to remove blocks of code at compilation time. It has no attributes, though you can use this tag in conjunction with the `jsfc` attribute.

This tag provides a way to remove parts of the document used during development or testing when the application goes into production, allowing to retain these bits of code for use later if further development or bug fixes are needed.

```
<ui:remove>
        This will be removed.
</ui:remove>
This will survive
<div jsfc="ui:remove">
This will be removed too
<h:outputText value="#{backingBean.andThisToo}"/>
</div>
And this will survive too!
```

Most of the content of the previous snippet won't appear in the final output:

```
This will survive
This will survive too!
```

You may wonder why we are not using normal HTML comments (`<!-- -->`) to remove the content from the final page, as what we put between the comment won't be visible to the user. Facelets will interpret the EL expressions within the comments unless the context parameter `facelets.SKIP_COMMENTS` is set to true in the `web.xml` file. In that case, the behavior would be similar.

<ui:repeat/>

The `ui:repeat` tag is used to iterate over a list of objects, and we always recommend its use instead `c:forEach` from the JSTL Code tag library. Table 1-13 shows its attributes.

Table 1-13. UI Repeat Attributes

ATTRIBUTE NAME	REQUIRED	DESCRIPTION
value	Yes	EL expression that resolves to the `List` of objects to be iterated over
var	Yes	The literal name of the variable used to iterate over the collection

As an example take a look at Listing 1-19, where we use the repeat tag to iterate over a list of birds provided by a backing bean.

Listing 1-19. repeat-example.xhtml

```
...
    <ul>
        <ui:repeat var="bird"
                   value="#{birdDirectory.birds}">
            <li>#{bird.name}</li>
        </ui:repeat>
    </ul>
...
```

The relevant resulting output follows:

```
<ul>
    <li>Parrot</li>
    <li>Eagle</li>
</ul>
```

You can also use the `ui:repeat` tag with the `jsfc` attribute. The snippet in Listing 1-20 will produce the same output as Listing 1-19:

Listing 1-20. repeat-jsfc-example.xhtml

```
...
    <ul>
        <li jsfc="ui:repeat"
            var="bird"
            value="#{birdDirectory.birds}">
         #{bird.name}
        </li>
    </ul>
...
```

Caution   `ui:repeat` and `c:forEach` are different. `ui:repeat` is a render-time evaluation, whereas `c:forEach` is a build-time evaluation. `c:forEach` does not represent a component in Facelets (it is a `TagHandler`) and will never become part of the component tree. It is used to create the tree when the page is first referenced (when the request is not a postback), but after that, `c:forEach` will not do anything else. On the other hand, `ui:repeat` is implemented as a component in Facelets and is part of the component tree. As an example, you could develop a list of elements with a button to add more elements. If you used `forEach` for the iteration, the new elements would never be added when the button is clicked (which is a postback).

Creating Composition Components

One of the greatest features of Facelets is the ability to create lightweight composition components. We have shown you how to use the Facelets templating tags, and now, we will show you how easy it is to create custom and reusable components using those tags. In this section, you will also see how to register those components in a custom `taglib`, which you can use in any of your applications.

Facelets provides a simple and fast way to create reusable components using tag source files, which will define the components and fragments that will compose our new component.

Creating the inputTextLabeled Custom Component

The first demonstration component we are going to create is a combined `h:outputLabel` and `h:inputText` component, which we are going to call `inputTextLabeled`. As combining this functionality is really common in our applications, writing such a component will help us reuse code and simplify our pages.

We want the component to be used like this in the JSF documents:

```
<custom:inputTextLabeled
    label="Name"
    value="#{bird.name}" />
```

We are going to use the `custom` namespace for the components we create in these examples.

Creating the Tag Source File

The first step in creating the component is creating of the tag file. To have a clear organization of the files in our project, we will create a file named `InputTextLabeled.xhtml` under `/WEB-INF/facelets/components`:

```
$PROJECT
+- /WEB-INF
    +- /web.xml
    +- /faces-config
    +- /facelets
        +- /mycustom.taglib.xml
        +- /components
            +- /InputTextLabeled.xhtml
            +- [other tag files]
    +- /[xhtml documents]
```

The source file contains the code in Listing 1-21.

Listing 1-21. InputTextLabeled.xhtml

```
<!DOCTYPE html PUBLIC "-//W3C//DTD ➥
XHTML 1.0 Transitional//EN"
        "http://www.w3.org/TR/xhtml1/DTD/ ➥
xhtml1-transitional.dtd">
<html xmlns="http://www.w3.org/1999/xhtml"
      xmlns:ui="http://java.sun.com/jsf/facelets"
      xmlns:h="http://java.sun.com/jsf/html">
<ui:component>
    <h:outputLabel value="#{label}: ">
        <h:inputText value="#{value}"/>
    </h:outputLabel>
</ui:component>

</html>
```

The implementation is really simple. We have created an h:outputLabel component with a nested h:inputText, which is one of the ways to use these two components together (instead of nesting the components, you could use an id in the h:inputText and make the for attribute of the h:outputLabel referring to that id).

The source file shows the use of two EL expressions for the value of the h:outputLabel and h:inputText components. The value of the EL expressions matches the name of the attributes of the custom tag, so we use it on our page like so:

```
<custom:inputTextLabeled
    label="Name"
    value="#{bird.name}" />
```

The label attribute in the custom:inputTextLabeled component will be used as the value of the h:outputLabel, and the value attribute will be used as the value of the h:inputText.

Registering the Tag in the Tag Library

Now that we have our tag file, let's register it in a custom tag library. First, we will need to create the tag library file, which we are going to put in the /WEB-INF/facelets folder. We will arbitrarily call it mycustom.taglib.xml; see Listing 1-22.

Listing 1-22. mycustom.taglib.xml

```
<!DOCTYPE facelet-taglib PUBLIC
        "-//Sun Microsystems, Inc.//DTD ➥
Facelet Taglib 1.0//EN"
        "http://java.sun.com/dtd/ ➥
facelet-taglib_1_0.dtd">

<facelet-taglib>
    <namespace>http://myfaces.apress.com/custom ➥
</namespace>

    <tag>
        <tag-name>inputTextLabelled</tag-name>
        <source>components/InputTextLabeled.xhtml
</source>
    </tag>

</facelet-taglib>
```

We have decided to call the tag library namespace http://myfaces.apress.com/custom, and we will need to declare this namespace in any pages where we are using the custom component.

After the namespace definition, we can find the tag element that defines our brand new tag. The tag-name element refers to the name we want to give to the tag, which in our case is inputTextLabeled. The source element contains the relative path to the tag file.

The next step is to tell Facelets that we want to use this library in our pages. To do so, we need to declare the library file in the `facelets.LIBRARIES` context parameter in the `web.xml` file shown in Listing 1-23.

Listing 1-23. web.xml

```xml
<context-param>
        <param-name>facelets.LIBRARIES</param-name>
        <param-value>
/WEB-INF/facelets/mycustom.taglib.xml
</param-value>
    </context-param>
...
```

And now we are ready to use the tag in our pages! As you can see, creating a new composite component with a tag and registering it is a fairly simple process.

Using the Tag

To use the tag we have created in a JSF page, we just need to declare the namespace in the top of the page and use the component. For instance, we could have a simple form to create new birds:

```xml
<!DOCTYPE html
        PUBLIC "-//W3C//DTD XHTML 1.0 Transitional//EN"
        "http://www.w3.org/TR/xhtml1/DTD/ ➥
xhtml1-transitional.dtd">
<html xmlns="http://www.w3.org/1999/xhtml"
      xmlns:ui="http://java.sun.com/jsf/facelets"
      xmlns:f="http://java.sun.com/jsf/core"
      xmlns:h="http://java.sun.com/jsf/html"
      xmlns:custom="http://myfaces.apress.com/custom">
<body>

<f:view>
    <h:form>
        <h:panelGrid columns="1">
```

```
            <custom:inputTextLabeled ⮱
label="Name" value="#{bird.name}"/>
            <custom:inputTextLabeled ⮱
label="Order" value="#{bird.order}"/>
            <custom:inputTextLabeled ⮱
label="Family" value="#{bird.family}"/>
              <h:commandButton ⮱
value="Add Bird" ⮱
actionListener="#{birdDirectory.addBird}"/>
          </h:panelGrid>
      </h:form>
  </f:view>
  </body>
</html>
```

Creating the simpleColumn Custom Component

The custom tag we are going to create now is `custom:simpleColumn`, which will simplify the creation of columns in a data table. It will define the header of the column and what to show in each cell, and we will use it like this:

```
<h:dataTable ...>
    <custom:simpleColumn ⮱
headerText="Name" ⮱
cellText="#{item.name}"/> ⮱
    ...
</h:dataTable>
```

Creating the Tag Source File

In this case, the source file for the tag is very simple too; see Listing 1-24. We create it in WEB-INF/facelets/components, with the rest of our custom components.

Listing 1-24. SimpleColumn.xhtml

```
<!DOCTYPE html PUBLIC "-//W3C//DTD ↪
XHTML 1.0 Transitional//EN"
        "http://www.w3.org/TR/xhtml1/DTD/ ↪
xhtml1-transitional.dtd">
<html xmlns="http://www.w3.org/1999/xhtml"
      xmlns:ui="http://java.sun.com/jsf/facelets"
      xmlns:f="http://java.sun.com/jsf/core"
      xmlns:h="http://java.sun.com/jsf/html">

<ui:composition>
    <h:column>
        <f:facet name="header">
            <h:outputText value="#{headerText}"/>
        </f:facet>
        <h:outputText value="#{cellText}"/>
    </h:column>
</ui:composition>

</html>
```

This case is very similar to the implementation used for
`custom:inputTextLabeled`. However, we are using `ui:composition`
here instead of `ui:component`, so no component instance will be added to
the JSF tree. Here too, we are using a couple of EL expressions
(`headerText` and `cellText`) that must match with the attributes of the
custom tag.

Registering the Tag in the Tag Library

Again, we need to register the custom tag in our `mycustom.taglib.xml`
file, shown in Listing 1-25.

```
<facelet-taglib>
    ...
    <tag>
        <tag-name>simpleColumn</tag-name>
        <source>components/SimpleColumn.xhtml</source>
    </tag>
    ...
</facelet-taglib>
```

The library should be already declared in the `facelets.LIBRARIES` context parameter in the `web.xml` file, because we did so for the previous custom tag.

Using the Tag

We could use our custom tag to replace any existing `h:column` in our applications, as shown in Listing 1-26.

Listing 1-26. simplecolumn-example.xhtml

```
<!DOCTYPE html
        PUBLIC "-//W3C//DTD XHTML 1.0 Transitional//EN"
        "http://www.w3.org/TR/xhtml1/DTD/ ↪
xhtml1-transitional.dtd">
<html xmlns="http://www.w3.org/1999/xhtml"
      xmlns:ui="http://java.sun.com/jsf/facelets"
      xmlns:f="http://java.sun.com/jsf/core"
      xmlns:h="http://java.sun.com/jsf/html"
      xmlns:custom="http://myfaces.apress.com/custom">
<body>

        <h:dataTable var="item" ↪
value="#{birdDirectory.allBirds}">
            <custom:simpleColumn ↪
headerText="Name"
cellText="#{item.name}"/> ↪
```

```
        <custom:simpleColumn headerText="Order"
cellText="#{item.order}"/>
        <custom:simpleColumn headerText="Family"
cellText="#{item.family}"/>
      </h:dataTable>

</body>
</html>
```

Clearly, the resulting page looks simpler and cleaner, and by reusing code (we don't have to declare the header facet all the time and so on), the maintenance is simplified.

Creating the scrollableDataTable Custom Component

Now it's time to start creating some cooler composition components. The one we are going to create now will be a composition of an h:dataTable and Tomahawk's t:dataScroller, so using the custom tag will produce tables with scrolling capabilities. To create such a table, we will only need to write this piece of code in our pages:

```
<custom:scrollableDataTable id="table1"
value="#{birdDirectory.allBirds}">
...
</custom:scrollableDataTable>
```

Creating the Tag Source File

In the tag file, we are going to use one h:dataTable and two t:dataScroller components, one to create navigation between table pages and the other to show contextual information about the rows shown to the user.

Note In this example, we are using the MyFaces Tomahawk library of components. As we mentioned earlier, Facelets does not include support for Tomahawk out of the box, and at the time of this writing, Tomahawk does not include a default tag library file in its JAR file. Therefore, we will need to create such a tag library or download an existing tag library for Tomahawk from the Internet, which is an easier option. A useful place to check on Facelets support for Tomahawk is in the MyFaces wiki pages (http://wiki.apache.org/myfaces/Use_Facelets_with_Tomahawk).

In our WEB-INF/facelets folder, we now include the tomahawk.taglib.xml file, which, at least for this example's purposes, should include the tag for t:dataScroller; see Listing 1-27.

Listing 1-27. tomahawk.taglib.xml

```
<!DOCTYPE facelet-taglib PUBLIC
  "-//Sun Microsystems, Inc.//DTD ➥
Facelet Taglib 1.0//EN"
  "http://java.sun.com/dtd/facelet-taglib_1_0.dtd">

<facelet-taglib>
    <namespace>http://myfaces.apache.org/tomahawk
</namespace>

   ...
   <tag>
       <tag-name>dataScroller</tag-name>
       <component>
           <component-type>
org.apache.myfaces.HtmlDataScroller</component-type>
           <renderer-type>
```

```
org.apache.myfaces.DataScroller</renderer-type>
      </component>
  </tag>
  ...

</facelet-taglib>
```

Now, we are ready to use the `dataScroller` in our tag files. As we have done with the previous custom tags, we create the source file under `WEB-INF/facelets/components`, and this time, we name it `ScrollableDataTable.xhtml`; see Listing 1-28.

Listing 1-28. ScrollableDataTable.xhtml

```
<!DOCTYPE html PUBLIC "-//W3C//DTD ↪
XHTML 1.0 Transitional//EN"
       "http://www.w3.org/TR/xhtml1/DTD/ ↪
xhtml1-transitional.dtd">
<html xmlns="http://www.w3.org/1999/xhtml"
      xmlns:ui="http://java.sun.com/jsf/facelets"
      xmlns:f="http://java.sun.com/jsf/core"
      xmlns:h="http://java.sun.com/jsf/html"
      xmlns:t="http://myfaces.apache.org/tomahawk">

<ui:component>

    <h:dataTable id="#{id}" var="item" ↪
value="#{value}" rows="10">
        <ui:insert/>
    </h:dataTable>

          <h:panelGrid columns="1">

            <t:dataScroller
                   for="#{id}"
                   fastStep="10"
                   pageCountVar="pageCount"
                   pageIndexVar="pageIndex"
```

```
                        paginator="true"
                        paginatorMaxPages="9"
paginatorActiveColumnStyle="font-weight:bold;"
                        immediate="true">
                </t:dataScroller>

                <t:dataScroller
                    for="#{id}"
                    rowsCountVar="rowsCount"
                    displayedRowsCountVar="rowCountVar"
                    firstRowIndexVar="firstRowIndex"
                    lastRowIndexVar="lastRowIndex"
                    pageCountVar="pageCount"
                    immediate="true"
                    pageIndexVar="pageIndex">

            <h:outputFormat
value="Total {0}. ↪
Displaying {1} rows, from {2} to {3}. ↪
Page {4}/{5}">
                    <f:param value="#{rowsCount}" />
                    <f:param
                      value="#{rowCountVar}" />
                    <f:param
                      value="#{firstRowIndex}" />
                    <f:param
                      value="#{lastRowIndex}" />
                        <f:param value="#{pageindex}" />
                        <f:param value="#{pagecount}" />
                    </h:outputFormat>
                </t:dataScroller>

            </h:panelGrid>
    </ui:component>

</html>
```

The `h:dataTable` component used contains only a nested `ui:insert` component. Hence, whatever we put as nested content for our custom tag will appear as a child of `h:dataTable`, so we can insert the columns as we would do normally.

Next, we have the two `dataScroller` components. Both have the `for` attribute pointing to the `id` of the `dataTable`, which is defined by an EL expression. We will need to provide an `id` attribute in our custom tag. We could have decided to hard-code the `id` in the source tag, but in that case, we would only be able to use one `custom:scrollableDataTable` per page.

Note that we cannot use an EL expression for the `var` attribute of the `dataTable`. In the previous example, the value for the `var` attribute value is `item` (it could have been `foobar` or any other arbitrary name). This means that whenever we use the variable `item` in any expression inside the table, we will be referring to each element from the collection or data model passed to the table in the `value` attribute.

Registering the Tag in the Tag Library

We add the custom tag to the `mycustom.taglib.xml`; see Listing 1-29.

Listing 1-29. mycustom.taglib.xml

```
<facelet-taglib>
    ...
    <tag>
        <tag-name>scrollableDataTable</tag-name>
        <source>components/ScrollableDataTable.xhtml
        </source>
    </tag>
    ...
</facelet-taglib>
```

Using the Tag

Now, we can start using our new fancy composite component by inserting the tag where we desire.

The following Listing 1-30 shows a small example where we use the composite component explained in the previous section. The custom scrollable table is used to show some of our famous birds.

Listing 1-30. scrollabledatatable-example.xhtml

```
<!DOCTYPE html
        PUBLIC "-//W3C//DTD XHTML 1.0 Transitional//EN"
        "http://www.w3.org/TR/xhtml1/DTD/ ➥
xhtml1-transitional.dtd">
<html xmlns="http://www.w3.org/1999/xhtml"
      xmlns:ui="http://java.sun.com/jsf/facelets"
      xmlns:h="http://java.sun.com/jsf/html"
      xmlns:custom="http://myfaces.apress.com/custom">
<body>
    <h:form>

        <custom:scrollableDataTable
                id="table1"
                value="#{birdDirectory.allBirds}">
            <custom:simpleColumn
                headerText="Name"
                cellText="#{item.name}"/>
            <custom:simpleColumn
                headerText="Order"
                cellText="#{item.order}"/>
            <custom:simpleColumn
                headerText="Family"
                cellText="#{item.family}"/>
            <h:column>
                <h:outputText value="Empty column"/>
            </h:column>
        </custom:scrollableDataTable>
```

```
        </h:form>
    </body>
</html>
```

As you can see, like in the standard `h:dataTable`, we can nest columns (be they `h:columns` or our custom columns). The rendered result will be completely different than the `h:dataTable` component's results though, as our custom `dataTable` will be paged and will have scrolling capabilities.

Creating the editableColumn Custom Component

When creating a tag, we can use other custom tags in our code. This is the case for the tag we are going to create now, `custom:editableColumn`, which render cells that can be edited:

```
<h:dataTable ...>
    <custom:editableColumn
        headerText="Name"
        cellText="#{item.name}"
        editMode="true"/>
    ...
</h:dataTable>
```

Creating the Tag Source File

The tag file is similar to the `custom:simpleColumn` one, as both contain columns with simple headers. Depending on the value of the `editMode` attribute, which must be a Boolean, an `h:outputText` or a `custom:inputTextLabeled` component will be shown. The tag source file is shown in Listing 1-31.

Listing 1-31. EditableColumn.xhtml

```
<!DOCTYPE html PUBLIC "-//W3C//DTD ➥
XHTML 1.0 Transitional//EN"
        "http://www.w3.org/TR/xhtml1/DTD/ ➥
```

```
xhtml1-transitional.dtd">
<html xmlns="http://www.w3.org/1999/xhtml"
      xmlns:ui="http://java.sun.com/jsf/facelets"
      xmlns:f="http://java.sun.com/jsf/core"
      xmlns:h="http://java.sun.com/jsf/html"
      xmlns:custom="http://myfaces.apress.com/custom">

<ui:composition>
    <h:column>
        <f:facet name="header">
            <h:outputText value="#{headerText}"/>
        </f:facet>
        <h:outputText value="#{cellText}"
                      rendered="#{!editMode}"/>

        <h:panelGroup rendered="#{editMode}">
           <custom:inputTextLabeled
              label="#{headerText}" value="#{cellText}"/>
        </h:panelGroup>

    </h:column>
</ui:composition>

</html>
```

Registering the Tag in the Tag Library

We add the custom tag to the `mycustom.taglib.xml`; see Listing 1-32.

Listing 1-32. mycustom.taglib.xml

```
<facelet-taglib>
    ...
    <tag>
        <tag-name>editableColumn</tag-name>
        <source>components/EditableColumn.xhtml</source>
    </tag>
    ...
</facelet-taglib>
```

Using the Tag

We could use the `editableColumn` tag in our `scrollableDataTable`, so we could edit the content of the table. For instance, we could have buttons to toggle between normal and edit mode as in Listing 1-33.

Listing 1-33. editablecolumn-example.xhtml

```
<!DOCTYPE html
        PUBLIC "-//W3C//DTD XHTML 1.0 Transitional//EN"
        "http://www.w3.org/TR/xhtml1/DTD/ ➡
xhtml1-transitional.dtd">
<html xmlns="http://www.w3.org/1999/xhtml"
      xmlns:ui="http://java.sun.com/jsf/facelets"
      xmlns:h="http://java.sun.com/jsf/html"
      xmlns:custom="http://myfaces.apress.com/custom">
<head>
    <title>custom:simpleColumn</title>
</head>
<body>
    <h:form>

        <custom:scrollableDataTable
          id="table2" value="#{birdDirectory.allBirds}">
            <custom:simpleColumn
                headerText="Name"
                cellText="#{item.name}"/>
            <custom:editableColumn
                headerText="Order"
                cellText="#{item.order}"
                editMode="#{userBean.editMode}"/>
            <custom:editableColumn
                headerText="Family"
                cellText="#{item.family}"
                editMode="#{userBean.editMode}"/>
        </custom:scrollableDataTable>
```

```
    <h:commandButton value="Edit Mode"
     actionListener="#{userBean.switchToEditMode}"
     rendered="#{!userBean.editMode}"/>
    <h:commandButton value="Normal Mode"
     actionListener="#{userBean.switchToNormalMode}"
     rendered="#{userBean.editMode}"/>
   </h:form>
 </body>
 </html>
```

Cool, isn't it? And simple.

Reusing the Custom Tag Library

For our custom tags, we have directly created the necessary files under
WEB-INF/facelets. This means that our nice composite components can
only be used in one application. Of course, we can create a tag library that
can be used in many applications.

To do that, we could bundle everything in a JAR file that could have the
following structure:

```
$JAR_PROJECT
+- /META-INF
   +- /mycustom.taglib.xml
+- /tags
   +- InputTextLabeled.xhtml
   +- SimpleColumn.xhtml
   +- [other tag files]
```

In the /META-INF/mycustom.taglib.xml file, we would be registering
the tags like the one shown in Listing 1-34.

Listing 1-34. mycustom.taglib.xml

```
<!DOCTYPE facelet-taglib PUBLIC
        "-//Sun Microsystems, Inc.//DTD ➥
Facelet Taglib 1.0//EN"
```

```
            "http://java.sun.com/dtd/ ➥
facelet-taglib_1_0.dtd">

<facelet-taglib>
    <namespace>http://myfaces.apress.com/custom
    </namespace>

    <tag>
        <tag-name>inputTextLabeled</tag-name>
        <source>/tags/InputTextLabeled.xhtml
</source>
    </tag>
    <tag>
        <tag-name>scrollableDataTable</tag-name>
        <source>/tags/ScrollableDataTable.xhtml</source>
    </tag>
    ...

</facelet-taglib>
```

And you are ready to use your custom tag library in any application, as
Facelets will automatically search for tag library definitions in the META-
INF folder of the JAR files.

Using Source Files from Other JAR Libraries

You may wonder if it is possible to use the source tag files from other JAR
files when implementing your own component. This is possible by
providing a custom Facelets resource resolver. For instance, we could
extend the com.sun.facelets.impl.DefaultResourceResolver like in
this example:

```
public class SourceJarResolver
        extends DefaultResourceResolver
{
    public SourceJarResolver() {
        super();
    }
```

```java
public URL resolveUrl(String path)
{
    // delegate the default URL resolution
    // to the superclass
    URL url = super.resolveUrl(path);

    // if no URL is found, try to
    // get the resource from the classpath
    if (url == null)
    {
        // remove the starting forward slash
        // if found
        if (path.startsWith("/"))
        {
            path = path.substring(1);
        }

        // get the resource from the classpath
        url = Thread.currentThread()
                    .getContextClassLoader()
                    .getResource(path);
    }
    return url;
}

public String toString()
{
    return "SourceJarResolver";
}
}
```

In this custom resource resolver, we first try the default resolution by delegating to the superclass, and if no resource is found, we try to get the resource from the classpath.

To use this custom resolver, we need to register it in the `faces-config.xml` file:

```
<context-param>
    <param-name>facelets.RESOURCE_RESOLVER</param-name>
    <paramvalue>
        com.apress.myfaces.SourceJarResolver
    </param-value>
</context-param>
```

Extending Facelets

Like JSF, Facelets was designed with extensibility in mind. It has a simple and open architecture focused only on the creation of the component tree and interweaving of content. As Facelets only extends one part of JSF, it can be used with any other framework built on top of JSF.

Facelets Architecture

Facelets extends the `ViewHandler` class with the `FaceletViewHandler` to tweak the rendering behavior and the strategy for saving and restoring the view state. Facelets view creation follows the process outlined in this section.

First, the `FaceletViewHandler` creates a new `UIViewRoot` when there is a request for a new JSF page. The default behavior of JSF 1.1 (not 1.2) is to invoke the restore of the view in the first request, but the `FaceletViewHandler` skips this step and goes directly to render the view if using JSF 1.1.

If Facelets is not supposed to handle the request, the rendering will be delegated to the parent `ViewHandler`.

Before rendering the view, a Facelets instance is created by the `FaceletFactory` class that is used to populate the `UIComponent` elements of the view. To do this, the `UIViewRoot` is applied to the Facelets instance:

```
FacesContext faces = FacesContext.getCurrentInstance();
FaceletFactory factory = FaceletFactory.getInstance();
Facelet facelet = factory.getFacelet("/main.xhtml");
facelet.apply(faces, faces.getViewRoot());
```

Next, the `UIViewRoot` is rendered to the response, and the page is shown to the user. The essential information (e.g., form data) from the state of the tree is saved for subsequent requests. Inline text and other transient components are not stored.

When a subsequent request comes to the JSF application, the view is restored with the state information saved from the previous request. This view is then passed through the JSF life cycle, which will end, depending on the action that was fired, in the creation of a new view or a rerendering of the same view (if there where validation errors).

If the view is rerendered, the Facelets class is used to complement the restoring of the view with the unsaved inline text and transient components.

The `UIViewRoot` is then asked by the view handler to render itself to the response.

This process is repeated again when a new request comes.

The Facelets class's (`com.sun.facelets.Facelet`) only mission is to populate the component tree. It can be accessed at the same time by several threads, and it is compiled into memory, so it can be effectively shared by all the requests. Only one `com.sun.facelets.Facelet` instance exists per XML or XHTML resource.

Note   Optimized tree generation is one of the major advantages of Facelets over JSP. The purpose of JSP is to render output by generating a class that contains a long list of `out.println()` methods. In JSF, JSP is used to create the component tree by encapsulating the rendered output into components along with the JSF ones. As we are interested in building the tree, Facelets is more optimal than JSP, as it was designed particularly for this purpose.

Once the Facelets instance is applied to the `UIViewRoot`, the component tree is populated. The logic to populate the tree is delegated to an internal tree of participants, implementations of `FaceletHandler` (`com.sun.facelets.FaceletHandler`), created by the Facelets compiler. They participate in the tree creation by receiving `UIComponent` elements and processing them accordingly.

The `FaceletHandler` interface is very simple and just contains a method to apply some behavior when the `UIComponent` is passed:

```
public void apply(FaceletContext ctx,
                  UIComponent parent)
        throws IOException, FacesException,
               FaceletException, ELException;
```

You will see in the next section how a `FaceletHandler` can be used to define the behavior of the tags and components that are part of the Facelets framework.

Custom Tag Development

The `TagHandler` is an essential element in the Facelets framework. Facelets builds a stateless tree of `TagHandler` components shared by all request to coordinate the building of the `UIComponent` objects.

The `TagHandler` components have the logic to decide whether the body of a tag should be added to the component tree.

Note   A `TagHandler` is effective for all events other than postbacks. On postback, the tree is not rebuilt.

The attributes of a tag are defined in the `TagHandler` and not in a separate XML or `*.tld` file like for JSP.

As an example, let's create a `TagHandler` that calculates a random number and puts it into the context so it can be reused in the page. The code for the `RandomGeneratorTagHandler` could be something like this:

```
public class RandomGeneratorTagHandler
        extends TagHandler
{
    private TagAttribute min;
    private TagAttribute max;
    private TagAttribute var;

    public RandomGeneratorTagHandler  ➥
            (TagConfig tagConfig)
    {
        super(tagConfig);

        // min attribute
        this.min = getAttribute("min");

        // max attribute
        this.max = getAttribute("max");

        // var attribute
        this.var = getRequiredAttribute("var");
    }
```

```java
public void apply(FaceletContext faceletContext,
              UIComponent parent)
        throws IOException, FacesException,
              FaceletException, ELException
{
        int minValue = Integer.MIN_VALUE;
        if (this.min != null)
        {
            minValue = min.getInt(faceletContext);
        }

        int maxValue = Integer.MAX_VALUE;
        if (this.max != null)
        {
            maxValue = max.getInt(faceletContext);
        }

        int randomNum =
          new Random().nextInt(maxValue)+ minValue;

        faceletContext.setAttribute
         (var.getValue(faceletContext), randomNum);
        this.nextHandler.apply(faceletContext,
         parent);
    }
}
```

As we you see in the previous snippet, our class extends the foundation abstract class `TagHandler` and implements its abstract method, `apply(FaceletContext,UIComponent)`. In the constructor, we have defined the three possible variables that this handler is going to accept:

- `min`: This optional attribute defines the minimum random number. By default, the value is `Integer.MIN_VALUE`.

- `max`: This optional attribute defines the maximum random number. By default, the value is `Integer.MAX_VALUE`.

- `var`: This attribute is required. It is the name of the variable that will be set with the random attribute. In our page, we will use this variable name when using this attribute.

We use the method `getAttribute()` or `getRequiredAttribute()` to get the appropriate attribute from the list of attributes passed to the tag in a JSF page. The `getRequiredAttribute()` method checks if the attribute has been used and throws an exception if it has not.

In the `apply(FaceletContext,UIComponent)` method, we implement the behavior of the tag. We check if the `min` and `max` attributes are null, initializing them to the minimum and maximum values if that is the case. Next, we generate the random value and set it to the `FaceletContext`, so it can be used by other tags in the page. Finally, we invoke the apply method for the subsequent Facelets handler to continue generating the tree for the children of the tag.

Once we have implemented the tag handler, we need to register it in the tag library. We need to use the `handler-class` element to point to the tag handler we have created, as shown in Listing 1-35.

Listing 1-35. mycustom.taglib.xml

```xml
<facelet-taglib>
 <namespace>http://myfaces.apress.com/custom
</namespace>
 ...
    <tag>
        <tag-name>random</tag-name>
        <handler-class>
            com.apress.myfaces.RandomGeneratorTagHandler
        </handler-class>
    </tag>
 ...
</facelet-taglib>
```

In our view document, we would use the tag like in this snippet:

```xml
<custom:random var="randomValue" min="0" max="10">
        <h:outputText
            value="Random number: #{randomValue}"/>
  </custom:random>
```

The preceding snippet would output something like this:

```
Random number: 6
```

Using Metatags

In some cases, attributes need to be set in a special way. For instance, a specialized component with an attribute must be evaluated to a method with a specific signature. Facelets provides the class `com.sun.facelets.tag.MetaTagHandler`, and we can extend it to use its automatic wiring capabilities for setting these special attributes. This class, which itself extends from `TagHandler`, uses a few objects to coordinate the wiring:

- `MetaData`: This defines how to wire dynamic or literal state into the passed `Object`.

- `MetaDataTarget`: This determines how and which `MetaData` will be wired in a `MetaRule`.

- `MetaRule`: This defines the rule for `MetaData` on the passed `MetaDataTarget`.

- `MetaRuleset`: This mutable set of rules will be used in automatically wiring state to a particular object instance. Rules assigned to this object will be composed into a single `MetaData` instance.

The `MetaDataHandler` declares two methods, which can be extended: `setAttributes(FaceletContext,Object)` and `createMetaRuleset(Class)`. The first method will be invoked by the subclasses according to the set of rules (`MetaRuleset`) created by the second method.

As you have seen in previous sections, if we create a custom tag handler, we will need to register it by using the `handler-class` element in the tag library.

The Facelets API provides three implementations of the `MetaTagHandler` that can be customized to automatically wire the attributes in components, converters, or validators. We are going to see these in the following sections.

Custom ComponentHandlers

Wiring in components can be customized by extending the `com.sun.facelets.tag.jsf.ComponentHandler` class. One of the implementations already provided by Facelets is `HtmlComponentHandler`:

```
public class HtmlComponentHandler
        extends ComponentHandler {
    public HtmlComponentHandler
                (ComponentConfig config)
    {
        super(config);
    }
```

```
    protected MetaRuleset
            createMetaRuleset(Class type) {
        return super.createMetaRuleset(type)
                    .alias("class", "styleClass");
    }
}
```

In the `HtmlComponentHandler`, the `createMetaRuleset` method is overridden to wire the alias attribute to the `styleClass` bean property. If we want to enable the automatic wiring for an existing component, we need to register the handler in the `taglib`, associating it with the component:

```
<facelet-taglib>
<namespace>
    http://myfaces.apress.com/custom
</namespace>
...
    <tag>
        <tag-name>anotherTag</tag-name>
        <component>
          <component-type>
            com.apresss.myfaces.SomeComponent
          </component-type>
          <renderer-type>
            com.apresss.myfaces.SomeComponentRenderer
          </rendere-type>
          <handler-class>
            com.apresss.myfaces.HtmlComponentHandler
          </handler-class>
        </component>
    </tag>
...
</facelet-taglib>
```

Once we've compiled the preceding code, when using the `anotherTag` in our page, the attribute class would be wired to the attribute `styleClass` of `SomeComponent`.

Let's now look at a more complex example not provided by Facelets: the component handler needed by the Tomahawk's `inputSuggestAjax` component (at the time of this writing, this handler is in the sandbox). The following example shows how to make it work properly in Facelets:

```
public class InputSuggestAjaxComponentHandler
                        extends HtmlComponentHandler
{
    private TagAttribute maxSuggestedItems;

    public InputSuggestAjaxComponentHandler ↪
            (ComponentConfig tagConfig) {
        super(tagConfig);

        maxSuggestedItems =
                getAttribute("maxSuggestedItems");
    }

    protected MetaRuleset createMetaRuleset(Class type)
    {
        MetaRuleset metaRuleset =
            super.createMetaRuleset(type);
        Class[] paramList =
            (maxSuggestedItems != null) ?
                new Class[]{String.class, Integer.class} :
                new Class[]{String.class};
        MetaRule metaRule =
                new MethodRule("suggestedItemsMethod",
                                List.class, paramList);

        metaRuleset.addRule(metaRule);

        return metaRuleset;
    }
}
```

The `inputSuggestAjax` tag contains the `suggestedItemsMethod` attribute, which accepts an EL method expression. The expression must evaluate to a method in a backing bean, which is the method that provides suggestions to the component based on a prefix (whatever the user has already introduced in the field rendered by the component). Optionally, the method invoked can contain a second parameter, corresponding to the value of the `maxSuggestedItems` attribute, to limit the amount of suggestions returned by the method.

To do the wiring, in the component tag handler, we override the `createMetaRuleSet` method to return a set with a `MetaRule` for the method we want to invoke. We use the `MetaRule`'s extension `MethodRule`, where we define the name of the attribute, the type returned, and an array of parameter types. As the method we need to invoke has two variations, depending on the presence of the `maxSuggestedItems` attribute, the size of the array of parameter types is variable.

Finally, we need to register the tag, as shown in Listing 1-36.

Listing 1-36. tomahawk-sandbox.taglib.xml

```
...
<tag>
        <tag-name>inputSuggestAjax</tag-name>
        <component>
            <component-type>
                org.apache.myfaces.InputSuggestAjax
            </component-type>
            <renderer-type>
                org.apache.myfaces.InputSuggestAjax
            </renderer-type>
            <handler-class>
    com.apress.myfaces.InputSuggestAjaxComponentHandler
            </handler-class>
        </component>
    </tag>
...
```

Custom ConvertHandlers

As the `MetaTagHandler` can wire attributes on any instance of `Object`, not just `UIComponents` like in the previous example, we can use it to implement custom validators by extending `com.sun.facelets.tag.jsf.ConvertHandler`. For example, we can find the class `com.sun.facelets.tag.jsf.core.ConvertNumberHandler` in the API:

```
public final class ConvertNumberHandler
                             extends ConvertHandler
{

    private final TagAttribute locale;

    public ConvertNumberHandler(TagConfig config)
    {
        super(config);
        this.locale = this.getAttribute("locale");
    }

    /**
     * Returns a new NumberConverter
     */
    protected Converter createConverter
                    (FaceletContext ctx)
                throws FacesException, ELException,
                    FaceletException
    {
        return ctx.getFacesContext().getApplication()
          .createConverter(NumberConverter.CONVERTER_ID);
    }

    protected void setAttributes
                    (FaceletContext ctx, Object obj)
```

```
    {
        super.setAttributes(ctx, obj);
        NumberConverter c = (NumberConverter) obj;
        if (this.locale != null) {
            c.setLocale(ComponentSupport.getLocale(ctx,
                        this.locale));
        }
    }

    protected MetaRuleset createMetaRuleset
                            Class type)
    {
        return super.createMetaRuleset(type)
                .ignore("locale");
    }
}
```

This example implements custom wiring for the `locale` attribute in the `setAttributes(Faceletscontext,Object)` method. As we are taking care of the handling of the locale, we can tell the `createMetaRuleset(Class)` method to ignore that attribute. The other properties of the `NumberConverter` will be treated normally.

Custom ValidateHandlers

We can wire validators too, by extending `com.sun.facelets.tag.jsf.ValidateHandler`. There is a default implementation in the Facelets API, which is the `com.sun.facelets.tag.jsf.core.ValidateDelegateHandler`:

```
public final class ValidateDelegateHandler
                            extends ValidateHandler
{

    private final TagAttribute validatorId;

    public ValidateDelegateHandler(TagConfig config)
    {
```

```java
        super(config);
        this.validatorId =
            this.getRequiredAttribute("validatorId");
    }

    /**
     * Uses the specified "validatorId"
     * to get a new Validator instance from the
     * Application.
     *
     */
    protected Validator createValidator
                          (FaceletContext ctx)
    {
        return ctx.getFacesContext()
                .getApplication()
                .createValidator(
                    this.validatorId.getValue(ctx));
    }

    protected MetaRuleset
            createMetaRuleset(Class type)
    {
        return super.createMetaRuleset(type).ignoreAll();
    }
  }
}
```

As we are doing all the attribute mapping ourselves, we can call the `ignoreAll()` method for the `MetaRuleset` too.

Extending the ViewHandler

The Facelets `ViewHandler` (`com.sun.facelets.FaceletViewHandler`) can be extended as well. It also has many protected methods that can be overridden, so you can tweak the initialization, compiler selection, response writer, response encoding, view rendering, and more.

To extend the `ViewHandler`, we need to provide the view handler class in the `faces-config.xml` file:

```
faces-config>
    <application>
        <view-handler>
            com.sun.facelets.MyExtendedFaceletViewHandler
        </view-handler>
    </application>
...
</faces-config>
```